Afia Visits the Bronx Zoo

AFIA VISITS THE BRONX ZOO
Copyright © 2021 Yaa Asare
All Right Reserved

All rights reserved. This book or any part of it may not be reproduced, distributed, transmitted or used in any way without the written permission of the copyright owner, except in the case of brief quotations in a book review and other noncommercial uses allowed by copyright law.
To request permissions, contact the author at
Yasreus@yahoo.com

Printed in the United States of America
ISBN: 978-1-7365589-0-4 (Paperback)
ISBN: 978-1-7365589-2-8 (Hardback)
ISBN: 978-1-7365589-1-1 (ebook)

Written by Yaa Asare
Illustrated by Lidya Riani

Afia Visits the Bronx Zoo

A day at the Bronx Zoo is always so much fun! Afia lives near the zoo, so she visits often with her parents.

She jumps up and down with excitement as she watches the gorillas jump around.

She shouts, "Bye bye, gorillas!" when they leave.

She hugs her mommy and daddy when she sees a baby monkey hugging its mommy.

She shouts, "Mommy, look!" whenever she sees a monkey jumping from one tree to another.

The African plains is where Afia sees zebras and lions.

Seeing one of the lions sleeping on a rock makes Afia a little sleepy herself.

She yawns and asks her daddy to pick her up.

"Lions didn't roar today", Afia whispers to her dad with a sad face.

She rests on her father's shoulders as they leave the African plains.

Afia always goes to the butterfly garden.

At the farm yard, she gets to feed the animals.

She never stops laughing while riding on the camel.

Afia ends her day with an adventure at the nature trek.

It is so much fun to walk, climb, and crawl on netted bridges, tunnels, and wiggly surfaces.

Milton Keynes UK
Ingram Content Group UK Ltd.
UKHW050054110124
435831UK00003B/16